THE SCOOBY-DOO! COOKBOOK

Kid-Friendly RECIPES for the WHOLE GANG

by Katrina Jorgensen

CAPSTONE EDITIONS
a capstone imprint

T0019655

Published by Capstone Editions, an imprint of Capstone.
1710 Roe Crest Drive
North Mankato, Minnesota 56003
www.capstonepub.com

Library of Congress Cataloging-in-Publication Data
is available on the Library of Congress website.

ISBN: 978-1-68446-147-9 (hardcover)
ISBN: 978-1-68446-148-6 (paperback)
ISBN: 978-1-68446-149-3 (ebook PDF)

Summary: Guaranteed to solve any case of hunger! This
official Scooby-Doo cookbook features—Zoinks!—more
than 25 kid-friendly recipes from the Mystery Inc. gang,
including Scooby's favorite treats, Shaggy's must-have
cheese-and-pickles pizza, jaw-stretcher sandwiches, and
healthy dog biscuits for your own hungry pup. Jam-
packed with step-by-step photos, cooking basics, and
fun facts from the ever-popular show, The Scooby-
Doo! Cookbook is sure to please fans of all ages, from
meddling kids to adults. Rummy!

Illustrations
Provided by Warner Bros.

Photo Credits
Capstone: Karon Dubke

Design Elements
Shutterstock: Omeris, Vriens Imagineering

Editorial Credits
Editor: Mari Bolte; Designer: Sarah Bennett; Food Stylist:
Sarah Schuette; Media Researcher: Morgan Walters;
Production Specialist: Kathy McColley

Contents

Basic Kitchen Rules 4

Swamp Brownie Cocoa 6

Donut Demon 8

Mystery Machine Road Trip To-Go Cups 10

Attack Snacks 12

Saturday Morning Cartoon Cakes 14

Marshmallow Man Cereal Bars 16

Toasty Ghosties 18

Mystery Map Pizza 20

The Gang's Mac 'n Cheese Volcano 22

SD Delivery Dogs 24

The World's Biggest Green Burrito 26

Villain Mask Stacker Surprise 30

Coolsville Crisp Chips 32

Shaggy and Scooby's Jaw Stretcher Special 34

Shaggy Shake 36

Zoinks, It's, Like, a Huge Sandwich! 38

Lost My Glasses Lemonade 40

Scoopy-Doobie-Doo! 42

Jinkies! Juice Pops 44

Creepy Spooky Terror Land Churros 46

The Gang's All Here Cookies 48

Mystery Inc. Misty Drink 52

Shaggy's Chocolately Carnival Corn 54

Pawsome Punch 56

Wart Pudding Parfaits 58

Creepy Spooky Terror Land Cotton Candy Cupcakes ... 60

The Cake Monster Caper 62

Can't Get Enough? 64

Basic Kitchen Rules

Solve the mystery of how to cook safely in the kitchen with these rules.

1. Always use clean hands, tools, and surfaces to make your food.

2. Make sure you wash your hands and keep your tools and surfaces clean after touching meat that has not been cooked.

3. Some recipes use hot appliances like a stove or oven, or sharp tools like a knife or scissors. Ask an adult member of your gang to help with these tasks!

Using Metric Tools?

Here are conversions to make your recipe measure up.

¼ teaspoon	1.25 grams or milliliters
½ teaspoon	2.5 g or mL
1 teaspoon	5 g or mL
1 tablespoon	15 g or mL
¼ cup	57 g (dry) or 60 mL (liquid)
⅓ cup	75 g (dry) or 80 mL (liquid)
½ cup	114 g (dry) or 125 mL (liquid)
⅔ cup	150 g (dry) or 160 mL (liquid)
¾ cup	170 g (dry) or 175 mL (liquid)
1 cup	227 g (dry) or 240 mL (liquid)
1 quart	950 mL

Fahrenheit°	Celsius°
325°	160°
350°	180°
375°	190°
400°	200°
425°	220°
450°	230°

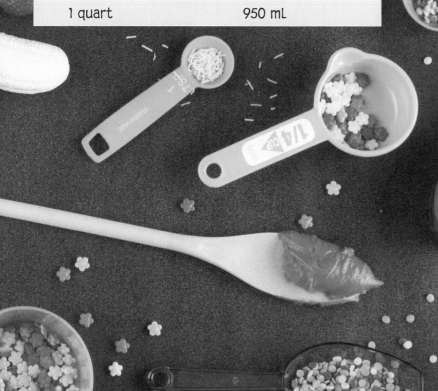

Swamp Brownie Cocoa

This Swamp Brownie Cocoa is a Scooby-and-the-gang favorite!
It's the perfect afternoon treat after a long day at Ghoul School.

Ingredients

1 tablespoon green sprinkles

1 tablespoon white chocolate powder

2 tablespoons sugar

¾ cup milk

green food coloring

½ teaspoon vanilla extract

whipped cream

rainbow sprinkles

pinch of cocoa powder

Steps

1. Spread the green sprinkles out on the plate.

2. Dip your finger in some water and rub your finger along the rim of the mug. Turn the mug upside down and dip into the green sprinkles.

3. In the liquid measuring cup, combine the white chocolate powder, sugar, 2 tablespoons of milk, and food coloring. Stir with a teaspoon until it makes a dark green paste.

4. Stir in the rest of the milk.

5. Microwave for 1 minute and 30 seconds or until hot. Stir in the vanilla.

6. Carefully pour into the mug. Top with whipped cream, rainbow sprinkles, and a pinch of cocoa powder.

Tools

small plate

mug

measuring spoons

microwave-safe liquid measuring cup

Tip If you can't find white chocolate powder, just use unsweetened cocoa powder instead.

Donut Demon

Scooby-Dooby DONUTS! Creative candy faces make plain-and-simple donuts frighteningly delicious! They're the perfect treat for any snack attack.

Ingredients

1 dozen plain donuts

two 12 ounce containers vanilla frosting

food coloring

assorted candies

Tools

bowls

butter knife

zip-top bags

scissors

Tip Use icing tips to add texture to your Donut Demons.

Steps

1. Place each donut flat on a clean surface.

2. Spread frosting from one can on each donut.

3. Scoop the rest of the frosting into zip-top bags. Each bag will be for one color.

4. Add food coloring to each bag. Close the bags and knead the frosting until the color is mixed in.

5. Cut a corner off each bag. Use the bags to squeeze frosting onto the donuts.

6. Use the candies to make each Donut Demon scary or special.

Mystery Machine
Road Trip To-Go Cups

The Mystery Machine has carried Fred, Daphne, Velma, Scooby, and Shaggy all over the world. The gang's got to eat while they're on the road! These to-go cups make the best early morning breakfast.

Ingredients

¼ cup butter

¼ cup peanut butter

green food coloring

½ cup banana, mashed

1 teaspoon vanilla extract

1 tablespoon honey

2 ½ cups old-fashioned oats

¼ cup crushed peanuts

¼ cup crushed almonds

¼ cup unsweetened
   coconut flakes

vanilla yogurt

fresh fruit

Tools

measuring cups and spoons

small saucepan

mixing spoon

large bowl

muffin tin

Steps

1. Ask an adult to preheat oven to 325 degrees. With his or her help, melt butter and peanut butter in a saucepan over medium heat.

2. Remove the pan from the heat and add the food coloring, banana, vanilla, and honey.

3. Combine the oats, nuts, and coconut in a large bowl. Pour the peanut butter mixture over, and stir to combine.

4. Measure about ¼ cup of the mixture into each of the muffin tin wells. Press the mixture into the tin, making sure it goes up the sides of the wells.

5. Ask an adult to bake the cups for 15 minutes. Remove from the oven and let cool.

6. Fill cups with yogurt and fruit. If you're not taking your cups on the road, add blueberry wheels for some tabletop fun!

Attack Snacks

Yikes! Running away from monsters is hard work!
Attack Snacks help Scooby and the gang stay ahead of
the ghosts through even the longest chase scenes.

Steps

1. Combine the Italian dressing mix and butter in a bowl until combined.

2. Stir the rest of the ingredients in a large mixing bowl. Drizzle butter mixture over.

3. Carefully stir to coat all the pieces.

4. Pour into a slow cooker and cook on low for 3 hours. Stir every hour, and then during the last 30 minutes, to prevent burning.

5. Scoop the mix onto a large baking sheet to fully cool.

6. Store in a sealed container up to 2 weeks.

Ingredients

1 envelope Italian dressing mix

½ stick (4 tablespoons) butter, melted

12 ounces mini pretzels

12 ounces corn chip cones

6 ounces mini saltine crackers

6 ounces cheese fish crackers

Tools

small mixing bowl

spoon

large mixing bowl

spatula

slow cooker

large baking sheet

Tip Don't have 3 hours to wait for crunchy deliciousness? Save time and do it in the microwave! Complete steps 1–3 in a large microwave-safe bowl. With an adult's help, microwave on high for 6 minutes, stopping to stir every 2 minutes. Then follow steps 5 and 6.

Saturday Morning Cartoon Cakes

Zoinks! These easy-to-make pancakes will have any breakfast fan flipping, especially when paired with a healthy helping of cartoons.

Steps

1. First, make the pancakes. Combine the pancake mix, egg, vanilla, and milk in a large mixing bowl. Whisk until just combined. It's okay if there are a few lumps!

2. Place the nonstick griddle on a burner. Ask an adult to turn the burner onto medium-high heat.

3. Use a measuring cup to scoop enough batter for six pancakes onto the griddle. When the pancakes bubble around the edges, it's time to flip them over with the spatula.

4. When the pancakes are golden brown, remove them from the griddle.

5. Set bananas, strawberries, and pineapple in the middle of a pancake.

6. Fold the pancake around the fruit and drizzle with Hot Fudge Sauce.

Ingredients

For the Pancakes:

1 cup pancake mix

1 egg

1 tsp vanilla

½ cup milk

sliced bananas, strawberries, and pineapple

Hot Fudge Sauce (recipe on page 43)

Tools

measuring cups and spoons

mixing bowl

whisk

nonstick griddle

spatula

Tip Everyone's heard of breakfast for dinner. What about dessert for breakfast? Make a sweet sandwich by stacking two pancakes around a scoop of raspberry sorbet. Then top with fruit and Hot Fudge sauce.

15

Marshmallow Man Cereal Bars

For a bad case of hunger, nothing beats these simple, ooey-gooey cereal bars—except maybe a double, triple-decker sardine and marshmallow fudge sandwich. Shaggy's favorite!

Steps

1. Place the butter in a large microwave-safe bowl. With an adult's help, heat for 45 seconds or until the butter is melted.

2. Add marshmallows. Stir with a spatula and then place the bowl back in the microwave. Heat for 1 minute. Stir until marshmallows are completely melted. Then add vanilla.

3. Pour the cereal into a large mixing bowl.

4. Drizzle the marshmallow mix over the cereal. Stir gently until all the cereal is coated.

5. Pour into the baking dish and press down with the spatula to pack the cereal tightly. Sprinkle the marshmallows in the small mixing bowl. Let cool before cutting.

Ingredients

½ cup butter

10 ounces mini marshmallows

1 teaspoon vanilla

7 cups oat cereal with marshmallow bits

Tools

measuring cups and spoons

large microwave-safe bowl

spatula

large mixing bowl

9.5-by-11-inch (24-by-28-cm) greased baking dish

Toasty Ghosties

Would you do it for a . . . cracker? These cheesy, salty, oh-so-effortless snacks will tempt even the scarediest dog to see who's hiding under that sheet.

Ingredients

- 8 ounces of grated sharp cheddar cheese
- 4 tablespoons cold butter, cut into small pieces
- ½ teaspoon salt
- ¼ teaspoon ground black pepper
- 1 cup flour
- 2 tablespoons cold water

Tools

- measuring cups and spoons
- food processor
- rolling pin
- cookie cutters
- parchment paper
- large baking sheet

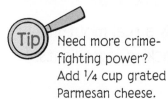 **Tip** Need more crime-fighting power? Add ¼ cup grated Parmesan cheese.

Steps

1. Ask an adult to preheat oven to 375 degrees.

2. Measure the cheese, butter, salt, and pepper into a food processor. With an adult's help, press the "pulse" button several times until the cheese and butter are small crumbs.

3. Add half of the flour and pulse again 5 or 6 times. Add the rest of the flour and repeat.

4. Pour in the water and hold down the "low" button until a ball of dough forms.

5. Have the adult place the dough on a clean surface. Roll it into a flat disc, about ⅛-inch (0.3-cm) thick. Use cookie cutters to cut out shapes.

6. Place on a parchment paper-lined baking sheet about an inch apart.

7. Bake for about 12 minutes or until the bottoms are just golden brown.

Mystery Map Pizza

Still searching for your favorite pizza toppings? Put down your Mystery Map. Try Shaggy's favorites: pickles and extra cheese. Rummy!

Steps

1. Ask an adult to preheat oven to 425 degrees.

2. Place pizza crust on a large baking sheet and set aside.

3. In a small mixing bowl, combine the olive oil, Italian seasoning, dried dill, salt and pepper, garlic powder, and onion powder. Blend together with a fork.

4. Use the pastry brush to brush the oil mixture over the top of the pizza crust. Be sure to get it all the way to the edges of the crust.

5. Sprinkle the cheese evenly on top of the pizza. Then add the pickles and bacon.

6. Ask an adult to help you place the pizza in the oven for about 10 to 12 minutes, or until the cheese is melted and bubbly.

7. With an adult's help, remove the pizza from the oven. Slice and serve while hot.

Ingredients

1 6-inch (16.4-cm) prebaked pizza crust

2 teaspoons olive oil

¼ teaspoon Italian seasoning

¼ teaspoon dried dill

pinch salt and pepper

¼ teaspoon garlic powder

¼ teaspoon onion powder

¼ cup mozzarella cheese

10 to 12 dill pickle slices

2 tablespoons crumbled cooked bacon

Tools

large baking sheet

small mixing bowl

measuring cups and spoons

fork

pastry brush

pizza cutter

Tip You can find prebaked pizza crust in the Italian section of your grocery store. Don't have pizza crust? That's okay! A flour tortilla or slice of pita bread works as a great backup. Veggie-based crusts are good gluten-free options.

The Gang's
Mac 'n Cheese Volcano

Open the mouth, between the gums, look out stomach, here it comes!
This souped-up macaroni explodes with molten, cheesy goodness.

Ingredients

10-ounce package frozen macaroni and cheese

4 tablespoons grated Monterey jack cheese

toppings such as Parmesan cheese, mini pepperonis, bacon crumbles, smoked sausage, diced ham, or peas

Tools

measuring spoons

two 6-ounce microwave-safe ramekins or bowls

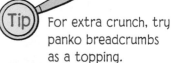

Tip For extra crunch, try panko breadcrumbs as a topping.

Steps

1. Place frozen macaroni and cheese in microwave. Ask an adult to cook on high for 4 minutes.

2. With an adult's help, remove from the microwave. Scoop about 3 tablespoons of macaroni and cheese into each ramekin.

3. Sprinkle 1 tablespoon of the shredded cheese in each ramekin.

4. Split the remaining macaroni between the two dishes and top with the rest of the cheese.

5. Put both ramekins back in the microwave. Have an adult cook on high for 1 minute.

6. Ask the adult to remove the ramekins. Then add your favorite toppings.

 # SD Delivery Dogs

Anytime, anywhere! Scooby and Shaggy would scarf down every type of hot dog known to human (or dog!)—from carnival-style corndogs to fire-roasted frankfurters to this Italian twist on a classic.

Ingredients

4 hot dogs

4 hot dog buns

½ cup marinara sauce

1 cup grated mozzarella cheese

½ teaspoon Italian seasoning

20 to 25 mini pepperonis

Tools

medium baking sheet

measuring cups and spoons

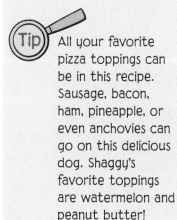

Tip All your favorite pizza toppings can be in this recipe. Sausage, bacon, ham, pineapple, or even anchovies can go on this delicious dog. Shaggy's favorite toppings are watermelon and peanut butter!

Steps

1. Ask an adult to preheat the oven on broil.

2. Set the hot dog buns on the baking sheet. Place a hot dog in each hot dog bun.

3. Spread marinara sauce evenly over each hot dog.

4. Place mozzarella cheese on each hot dog.

5. Sprinkle Italian seasoning over the cheese.

6. Decorate each hot dog with mini pepperonis.

7. With an adult's help, place the hot dogs in the oven for 3 to 4 minutes. Remove when the cheese is melted and a little brown.

The World's Biggest Green Burrito

Boy oh boy, this mucho grande Mexican creation is jam-packed with guacamole, ground beef, and refried beans. You could say, it's stuffed with enough stuff to make anyone stuffed!

Ingredients

For the Guacamole:

1 avocado

½ jalapeno, minced

½ medium onion, minced

1 tablespoon cilantro, chopped

1 tablespoon lime juice

½ teaspoon salt

For the Burritos:

1 pound ground beef

¾ cup salsa

1 packet taco seasoning

15-ounce can refried beans

4 burrito-sized flour tortillas

¾ cup cheddarjack cheese

Guacamole

sour cream, lettuce, tomatoes, extra salsa

Tools

knife

spoon

measuring cups and spoons

medium-sized bowl

fork

large skillet

cooking spoon

microwave-safe bowl

Tip Make the burrito vegetarian by leaving out the beef.

Steps

For the Guacamole:

1. Have an adult cut the avocado in half and remove the pit.

2. Use a spoon to scoop out the avocado flesh and place in a medium mixing bowl.

3. Add the jalapeno, onion, cilantro, lime juice, and salt.

4. Lightly mash the avocado with a fork until it is well blended with the other ingredients.

Jinkies!
Check it out—
burrito steps on the
next page! ☞

Steps, continued

For the Burritos:

1. Ask an adult to brown the ground beef in a skillet over medium heat. Drain off the fat.

2. Stir in the salsa and taco seasoning. Simmer for 5 minutes.

3. While it simmers, warm the refried beans in a microwave-safe bowl for 45 seconds.

4. Assemble the burritos. Use a spoon to spread about ¼ cup of the beans on each tortilla. Add about ½ cup of the meat mixture. Sprinkle 1 tablespoon of cheese over the meat.

5. Fold the top and bottom of the burrito in toward the center. Then roll up the burrito. Repeat for the rest of the tortillas.

6. Decorate the tops of the burritos with cheese, guacamole, sour cream, lettuce, tomatoes, and extra salsa.

Villain Mask Stacker Surprise

Now listen up, there is absolutely no such thing as a . . . BURGER MONSTER! Or, there won't be, once you've finished off this doggone good meal.

Ingredients

4 black bean burgers

2 leaves iceberg lettuce

2 thin slices red onion

2 slices white cheddar cheese

condiments such as ketchup, mustard, mayo, or relish

2 pickle slices

1 small pickle, cut in half

1 black olive, cut in half

1 black olive, cut into slices

1 cherry tomato, cut in half

Tools

kitchen shears

8 toothpicks

Tip Make each Burger Monster a little different! Decorate the eyes with vegetables, round cheese puffs, different colors of cheese circles, or blobs of mayonnaise and ketchup.

Steps

1. With an adult's help, cook the burgers according to package directions.

2. Place two patties on two plates. Add a leaf of lettuce and a slice of onion to the patty. Then top each with a second patty.

3. To make a mummy, cut strips out of a cheddar cheese slice. Cover your burger monster with strips. Add eyes using pickles, two olive pieces, and two squirts of mustard.

4. To make a scary monster, cut out fangs and two circles from the other cheese slice. Slide the cheese teeth between the patties. Add an olive slice for a tongue.

5. Place the cheese circles on top of the tomato halves to make eyes. Set a pickle half on the scary monster so it has a big eyebrow. Then add the cheese-and-tomato eyes.

6. Garnish the scary monster with your favorite condiments.

31

Coolsville Crisp Chips

Easy, cheesy, and oh-so delicious, these chips are
perfect for an afternoon snack—or a groovy beach party.

Ingredients

2 tablespoons cheddar cheese powder

1 tablespoon finely grated Parmesan cheese

1 teaspoon chili powder

1 teaspoon buttermilk powder

½ teaspoon salt

8-ounce bag kettle-cooked potato chips

2 tablespoons canola oil

Steps

1. Ask an adult to preheat oven to 425 degrees.

2. In a small bowl, mix the cheddar cheese powder, Parmesan cheese, chili powder, buttermilk powder, and salt. Set aside.

3. Spread out the chips on a large baking sheet. Ask an adult to place the baking sheet in the oven for 5 minutes.

4. Carefully transfer the potato chips to a large bowl. Drizzle the oil over the chips.

5. Sprinkle the powder mixture over the chips. Gently use the tongs to toss the chips around to coat.

Tools

measuring spoons

small bowl

large baking sheet

large mixing bowl

tongs

Tip You can find cheddar cheese powder by the popcorn toppings in your local grocery store.

Shaggy and Scooby's Jaw Stretcher Special

The name says it all! This supersized sandwich is a real mouthful, stacked with some of Shaggy's favorite lip-smacking ingredients.

Steps

1. Spread peanut butter and marshmallow fluff onto a slice of bread. Top with banana rounds and a second piece of bread.

2. With an adult's help, melt 1 tablespoon butter in a nonstick skillet. Set the sandwich on the skillet and cook until bread is golden brown.

3. While the sandwich cooks, spread hazelnut spread and jelly onto the third slice of bread. Top with chocolate chips.

4. Add 1 tablespoon butter to the skillet and flip the sandwich over. Carefully set the bread with the chocolate chips onto the sandwich, toppings-side-down.

5. When the bread on the bottom is golden brown, add 1 tablespoon butter to the skillet and flip the sandwich over again.

6. When all three pieces of bread have been toasted, remove the sandwich. Slice in half, and serve.

Ingredients

2 tablespoons peanut butter

2 tablespoons marshmallow fluff

3 slices sandwich bread

1 banana, sliced into rounds

3 tablespoons butter, softened

2 tablespoons hazelnut spread

2 tablespoons jelly

1 tablespoon chocolate chips

Tools

nonstick skillet

spatula

Shaggy Shake

The bravest heroes need to refuel after chasing monsters and bad-guy busting. This tripleberry shake is triple the taste and triple the yum!

Ingredients

mini marshmallows

2/3 cup vanilla ice cream

1/2 cup frozen tripleberry mix
(strawberries, blueberries,
raspberries)

2 tablespoons malted milk
powder

1/2 cup cold milk

whipped cream

sprinkles

sour candy strips

Tools

kitchen shears

tall glass

measuring cups and spoons

blender

wooden skewer

Tip No dairy in your diet?
That's okay! Sub out
equal parts of the
ice cream, malted
milk powder, and milk
with your favorite
nut, soy, or coconut
ice creams and milks.
Skip the whip and
decorate with extra
sugary sweets.

Steps

1. Cut the mini marshmallows in half. Press the cut
   ends inside the tall glass to make a polka dot
   pattern. Set aside.

2. Add the ice cream, berries, malted milk powder,
   and milk to a blender. Ask an adult to blend
   until smooth.

3. Pour the malt into the glass. Top with whipped
   cream and sprinkles.

4. Slide the candy strips onto the skewer to make
   a ribbon. Stick the skewer into the glass, with
   the candy facing up.

Zoinks, It's, Like, a Huge Sandwich!

Like Shaggy always says, "Let's do what we do best: Eat!"
Chowing down is the best—and only!—way to take down
this extra-large, Scooby-sized sandwich.

Ingredients

1 ounce bag plain potato chips

¼ cup cream cheese, softened

1 tablespoon honey mustard

4 slices sandwich bread

6 slices deli ham

3 slices cheddar cheese

3 leaves lettuce

3 slices tomato

6 dill pickle slices

Tools

small bowl

measuring cups and spoons

cutting board

chef's knife

Tip A long skewer can help keep these sandwiches together. Just watch out while you're chowing down!

Steps

1. Gently crush the potato chips inside the bag. Then open the bag and set aside.

2. Combine the cream cheese and honey mustard in a small bowl. Stir until smooth.

3. Spread cream cheese mixture onto one side of each bread piece.

4. Top three of the bread slices with a sprinkle of potato chips, 2 slices of ham, 1 slice of cheese, 1 piece of lettuce, 1 slice of tomato, and 2 dill pickle slices.

5. Stack the three bread slices on top of each other. Set the fourth slice of bread on top, cream cheese-side-down.

6. Have an adult help you cut your super sandwich into triangles.

Lost My Glasses Lemonade

You don't need glasses to enjoy ice-cold lemonade after a caper is complete. Relax now, search for specs after. (Sorry, Velma!)

Steps

1. Add sugar and water to a large saucepan. With an adult's help, cook over medium heat until the mixture begins to simmer and the sugar dissolves.

2. Pour the lemon juice into the saucepan and stir to combine. Let cool.

3. Add ice to pitcher.

4. Ask the adult to pour the lemon mixture over the ice.

5. Add the orange juice. Stir to combine.

6. Place ice and cherries in serving glasses before adding lemonade.

Ingredients

¾ cup sugar

4 cups water

⅔ cup lemon juice

2 cups ice

⅔ cup orange juice

additional ice for serving

maraschino cherries

Tools

measuring cups

large saucepan

2-quart pitcher

long spoon

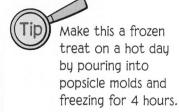

Tip Make this a frozen treat on a hot day by pouring into popsicle molds and freezing for 4 hours.

Scoopy-Doobie-Doo!

Just one more scoop. And then another one.
How about a few more? Any dessert lover is sure to
take down these chocolaty sweet sundaes lickety-split!

Ingredients

For the Hot Fudge Sauce:

1 cup sugar

1 cup heavy cream

1 cup cocoa powder

1 teaspoon vanilla extract

1 stick butter

pinch of salt

For the Sundae:

2 scoops vanilla ice cream
  or frozen yogurt

1/3 cup Hot Fudge Sauce

mini marshmallows

slivered almonds

whipped cream

1 maraschino cherry

Tools

measuring cups and spoons

saucepan

spoon

ice cream scoop

serving dish

Tip No nuts? If you have an allergy or just don't like nuts, you can switch out the almonds in favor of crumbled cookies, graham crackers, or pepitas.

Steps

1. For the Hot Fudge Sauce, combine the sugar, cream, cocoa powder, vanilla, butter, and salt in a saucepan. With an adult's help, heat over medium until everything is melted.

2. Pour the sauce into a heat-safe container. As it cools it will harden. You can heat it again if you need to. It will stay fresh for 1 week.

3. Scoop ice cream into a serving bowl. Drizzle hot fudge over the top.

4. Add rocks to your road! Top with mini marshmallows, slivered almonds, whipped cream, and a cherry.

Jinkies! Juice Pops

Loaded with fruity melon goodness, these juice pops
will make you say, "Jinkies!" This recipe makes
enough icy treats for the entire gang.

Steps

1. With an adult's help, peel the kiwis. Blend them with half of the fruit juice.

2. Pour the kiwi juice into popsicle molds. Freeze for 2 to 3 hours.

3. Put the watermelon and the rest of the fruit juice in a blender. Have an adult blend until smooth.

4. Pour the watermelon juice blend into popsicle molds. Place in the freezer.

5. After about 1 hour, remove the popsicles. Push popsicle sticks into the molds. Then return to the freezer for another 1 to 2 hours.

6. Remove from popsicle mold and enjoy!

Ingredients

4 kiwis

6 teaspoons fruit juice of your choice

4 cups seedless watermelon chunks

Tools

vegetable peeler

blender

measuring cups and spoons

popsicle mold

popsicle sticks

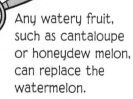

Tip Any watery fruit, such as cantaloupe or honeydew melon, can replace the watermelon.

Creepy Spooky Terror Land Churros

Jeepers! Eating these terrifyingly easy churros is just like visiting the Funland Amusement Park—but without the creepy, out-of-control robots, of course!

Ingredients

1 sheet puff pastry, thawed

1/2 stick butter, melted

3 tablespoons sugar

1 tablespoon ground cinnamon

green sanding sugar

Tools

parchment paper

large baking sheet

cutting board

pizza cutter

microwave-safe bowl

small mixing bowl

tongs

Tip For added yum, dip in the Hot Fudge Sauce on page 43.

Steps

1. Ask an adult to preheat oven to 450 degrees. Place a sheet of parchment paper on a large baking sheet and set aside.

2. Place the puff pastry on a large cutting board. Use the pizza cutter to slice the puff pastry into 16 equal sticks.

3. Place the sticks on the baking sheet, about 1/2-inch (1.3-cm) apart. Twist the sticks to make them look more like churros.

4. With an adult's help, place the baking sheet in the oven. Bake the sticks for 10 to 12 minutes.

5. Melt butter in a microwave-safe bowl. Set aside. Mix the sugar, cinnamon, and green sanding sugar in another bowl.

6. Have the adult remove the churros from the oven. Use the tongs to dip the top of a stick into the melted butter. Then dip into the cinnamon sugar. Repeat for the remaining churros. Serve immediately.

The Gang's All Here Cookies

Don't be afraid—use your hands to mix this dough!
These homemade (and handmade) cookies are perfect
for any meddling kids. Make one for each of the
Scooby Gang, or just decorate them for yourself.

Steps

1. Ask an adult to preheat oven to 350 degrees.

2. Unwrap the cookie dough and place in the mixing bowl. Add the flour. Use your hands to break up the dough and incorporate all the flour.

3. Set the cookie dough on a floured work surface. Ask an adult to roll the dough ¼-inch (0.6 cm) thick. Cut circles out of the dough.

4. Place the dough circles 1 inch (2.5 cm) apart on the greased baking sheet. Bake for 9 to 12 minutes or until the edges just begin to brown. Ask an adult to remove the cookies from the oven, and let cool completely before decorating.

5. Divide the vanilla frosting into the small bowls. Stir in food coloring to each bowl to represent a member of the Scooby Gang. Then use the knives to decorate the cookies, and add sprinkles.

Ingredients

roll of refrigerated sugar cookie dough

¼ cup flour, plus extra for work surface

1 container vanilla frosting

1 container chocolate frosting

yellow, red, blue, and green gel food coloring

blue, red, purple, green, orange, and teal confetti sprinkles

Tools

large baking sheet, greased

mixing bowl

mixing spoon

rolling pin

round cookie cutters

five small bowls

five knives

Jinkies!
Check it out—
decorating ideas on
the next page! ☞

Food coloring and sprinkles will help you create cookies that represent your favorite character!

FOR FRED COOKIES:

- yellow food coloring
- blue and red sprinkles

FOR DAPHNE COOKIES:

- red and blue food coloring (to make purple)
- green, orange, and purple sprinkles

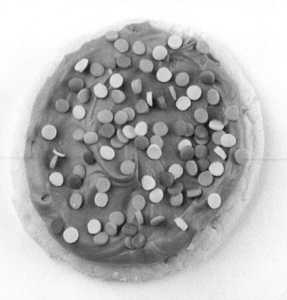

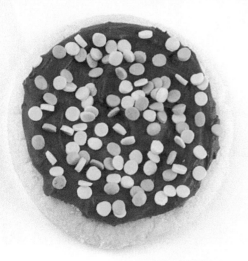

FOR SHAGGY COOKIES:
- chocolate frosting
- green sprinkles

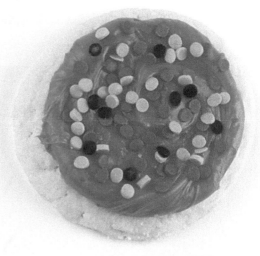

FOR VELMA COOKIES:
- red and yellow food coloring (to make orange)
- red, orange, and black sprinkles

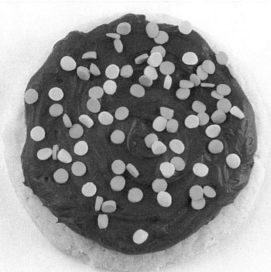

FOR SCOOBY COOKIES:
- chocolate frosting
- teal and yellow sprinkles

Mystery Inc. Misty Drink

What makes this drink so delicious? That's no mystery—the perfect blend of juices, with the addition of carbonated bubbles. Take a sip and get ready to bark, "Puppy power!"

Ingredients

orange

4 cups fruit punch, chilled

4 cups pineapple juice, chilled

25-ounce (750-milliliter) bottle sparkling apple cider

ice cubes

Tools

cutting board and knife

straws

measuring cups

gallon-sized pitcher

long spoon

tall glass

Tip Make it a punch party by pouring your Misty Drink in a large punch bowl. Add fresh or frozen fruit for added fun and flavor.

Steps

1. With an adult's help, slice the orange into rounds. Use a straw to cut out the center of each orange slice.

2. Combine the fruit punch, pineapple juice, and sparkling apple cider in a large pitcher. Gently stir to combine.

3. Pour into ice-filled glasses.

4. Slide orange slices onto the straws. Place an orange and straw into each glass. The orange should sit on top of the drink and hold the straw in place.

Shaggy's Chocolately Carnival Corn

Like Fred always says, "Let's split up, gang!"
Make enough of this super-sweet treat
to split with your friends.

Steps

1. Spread the popcorn on a parchment paper-lined baking sheet.

2. Place the chocolate chips with 1 teaspoon shortening in a microwave-safe bowl. With an adult's help, heat on high for 20 seconds. Stir. Repeat microwaving and stirring until the chocolate is melted and smooth.

3. Ask the adult to pour the chocolate mixture into a zip-top bag.

4. Snip the corner of the zip-top bag. Squeeze gently to drizzle the chocolate all over the popcorn.

5. Repeat steps 2–4 with teal candy melts.

6. Crumble the chocolate sandwich cookies. Sprinkle over the popcorn.

7. Drop sprinkles over the popcorn.

8. Allow to cool for 1 hour, then break into pieces and enjoy!

Ingredients

10 cups popped popcorn

1 cup semisweet chocolate chips

1 teaspoons shortening

1 cup teal candy melts

15 chocolate and peanut butter sandwich cookies

sprinkles

Tools

parchment paper

large baking sheet

measuring cups and spoons

microwave-safe bowls

spoon

zip-top bags

kitchen shears

Pawsome Punch

Scooby and Shaggy need all the energy they can get to teach at Ghoul School! A sip or two of Pawsome Punch is a refreshing relaxer after a long day of being in charge.

Ingredients

3 cups water

2 family-sized iced tea bags

2 cups peach nectar

1 cup cold water

peach puree

fresh peaches and raspberries

Tools

measuring cups

large saucepan

2-quart pitcher

shaped ice cube tray

Tip To add more color, pour different types of juice or fruit purees into the ice cube tray.

Steps

1. Pour the water into a large saucepan. Ask an adult to bring it to a boil.

2. Turn off the heat and add the tea bags. Let the tea steep for 15 minutes.

3. Pour the peach nectar and cold water into the pitcher. With an adult's help, add the tea.

4. Refrigerate for at least 2 hours.

5. Pour peach puree into the ice cube tray. Freeze for two hours or until frozen solid.

6. Pour tea mixture into drinking glasses. Top with shaped ice cubes, slices of fresh peach, and raspberries. Add a straw and enjoy!

Wart Pudding Parfaits

Wart Pudding sounds pretty yucky—but Scooby swears it's gourmet goo! Dig in and discover the secret to this monsterously tasty treat.

Steps

1. Place the graham cracker and malted milk balls in a zip-top bag. Close the top and crush into small pieces with the heavy object. Set aside.

2. Put half of the chocolate pudding in the bottom of the parfait dish or glass.

3. Sprinkle half of the graham cracker and malted milk ball mixture over the chocolate pudding.

4. Stir green food coloring into the vanilla pudding. Then scoop out the entire container of vanilla pudding into the glass.

5. Spread the remaining crushed graham cracker and malted milk balls on top of the vanilla pudding.

6. The rest of the chocolate pudding goes on top, followed by whipped cream.

7. Top the whipped cream with chocolate rice cereal bites, a whole malted milk ball, and green sprinkles.

Ingredients

1 graham cracker

8 malted milk balls, plus more for decorating

4-ounce cup prepared chocolate pudding

green food coloring

4-ounce cup prepared vanilla pudding

whipped cream

2 tablespoons chocolate rice cereal bites

green sprinkles

Tools

zip-top bag

heavy object, such as a mallet, rolling pin, or can

parfait dish or wide-rimmed glass

measuring spoon

Tip Swap out the vanilla pudding with butterscotch for a flavor twist.

Creepy Spooky Terror Land Cotton Candy Cupcakes

When in Funland (or anywhere, for that matter), cupcakes
are no joke! Baking is way less scary than exploring a haunted
amusement park, though. More sugar only makes them more fun!

Ingredients

Cake:

15.25-ounce box confetti
cake mix, plus ingredients
on package directions

Frosting:

12-ounce can white whipped
frosting

pink gel food coloring

blue gel food coloring

cotton candy

Tools

mixing bowls

measuring cup and spoons

muffin tin

cupcake liners

gallon zip-top bag

kitchen shears

small offset spatula or
butter knife

Tip For added colorful
fun, add 2 drops gel
food coloring to
your cake batter
before baking.

Steps

1. With an adult's help, make cupcakes according
   to the directions on the cake mix. After they
   are done baking, let cool completely.

2. Divide the frosting evenly between 2 small
   mixing bowls. Add 1 drop pink food coloring to
   one bowl. Mix well.

3. Add 1 drop blue food coloring to the other
   bowl of frosting. Mix well.

4. Drop frosting into the zip-top bag, alternating
   colors. Do not stir or smash bag.

5. Cut a corner off the zip-top bag. Squeeze
   frosting onto each cupcake.

6. Pull off pieces
   of cotton candy
   and decorate as
   you would like.

The Cake Monster Caper

Well gang, I guess that wraps up this mystery! Celebrate with another job well done with this no-bake spooky cake.

Ingredients

8-inch (20.3-cm) plain frosted layer cake, refrigerated

½ cup heavy cream

1 cup purple candy melts

1 cup lime green candy melts

chocolate sprinkles

candy eyes

Tools

large bowl

microwave-safe liquid measuring cup

microwave-safe bowls

fork

popsicle sticks

Tip Add more color to your Cake Monster by putting sprinkles over your cake while the candy melts are still wet.

Steps

1. Place the cake in a large bowl. Mash the cake and frosting together until it makes a dough.

2. Take a handful of the dough. Roll it between your hands until it forms a ball. Repeat until all the dough is used up. Press a popsicle stick into each ball. Refrigerate for 20 minutes.

3. With an adult's help, pour the cream into a liquid measuring cup. Microwave for 45 seconds. Do not let it boil.

4. Separate the candy melts into two microwave-safe bowls.

5. Microwave each bowl of melts according to package directions. Add ¼ cup of the cream to each, and stir with a fork until smooth.

6. Remove the cake balls from the refrigerator. Dip into the purple candy melts.

7. Use the green candy melts to give each monster hair. Sprinkle with chocolate sprinkles.

8. Press a candy eye onto each monster. Set the cake balls in the refrigerator until the candy melts have set.

CAN'T GET ENOUGH?

Find more Capstone titles to learn everything about the Mystery Inc. gang. Discover every villain Scooby, Shaggy, Daphne, Velma, and Fred have faced. See if you recognize any famous guest stars. Then learn the gang's favorite jokes! You'll feel like a member of the Scooby Gang yourself in no time.

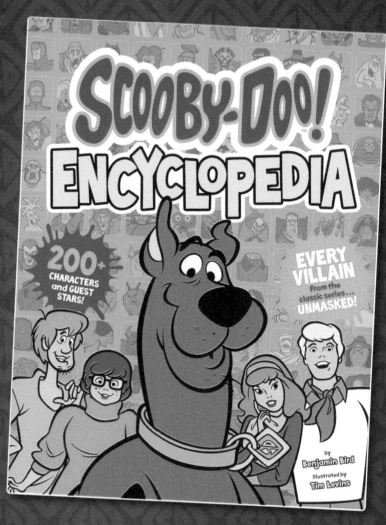

SCOOBY-DOO! ENCYCLOPEDIA

200+ CHARACTERS and GUEST STARS!

EVERY VILLAIN from the classic series... UNMASKED!

by Benjamin Bird

Illustrated by Tim Levins

SCOOBY-DOO! FOOD Jokes!

SCOOBY-DOO! ON THE GO Jokes!

SCOOBY-DOO! ANIMAL Jokes!

SCOOBY-DOO! MONSTER Jokes!